Date: 12/26/18

J 598 KOB
Kobasa, Paul A.,
Feathered animals /

Hello, Beautiful!

Feathered Animals

WORLD
BOOK

www.worldbook.com

World Book, Inc.
180 North LaSalle Street, Suite 900
Chicago, Illinois 60601
USA

For information about other World Book
publications, visit our website at
www.worldbook.com or call
1-800-WORLDBK (967-5325).

For information about sales to schools and
libraries, call 1-800-975-3250 (United States),
or 1-800-837-5365 (Canada).

Library of Congress Cataloging-in-Publication
Data for this volume has been applied for.

Hello, Beautiful!
ISBN: 978-0-7166-3567-3 (set, hc.)

Feathered Animals
ISBN: 978-0-7166-3572-7 (hc.)

Also available as:
ISBN: 978-0-7166-3582-6 (e-book)

Printed in China by Shenzhen Wing King Tong
Paper Products Co., Ltd., Shenzhen, Guangdong
1st printing July 2018

Staff

Writer: Paul A. Kobasa

Executive Committee

President
Jim O'Rourke

Vice President and
Editor in Chief
Paul A. Kobasa

Vice President, Finance
Donald D. Keller

Vice President, Marketing
Jean Lin

Vice President,
International Sales
Maksim Rutenberg

Vice President, Technology
Jason Dole

Director, Human Resources
Bev Ecker

Editorial

Director, New Print
Tom Evans

Managing Editor, New Print
Jeff De La Rosa

Senior Editor, New Print
Shawn Brennan

Editor, New Print
Grace Guibert

Librarian
S. Thomas Richardson

Manager, Contracts &
Compliance (Rights &
Permissions)
Loranne K. Shields

Manager, Indexing Services
David Pofelski

Digital

Director, Digital Content
Development
Emily Kline

Director, Digital Product
Development
Erika Meller

Manager, Digital Products
Jonathan Wills

Graphics and Design

Senior Art Director
Tom Evans

Senior Visual
Communications Designer
Melanie Bender

Media Researcher
Rosalia Bledsoe

**Manufacturing/
Production**

Manufacturing Manager
Anne Fritzinger

Proofreader
Nathalie Strassheim

Contents

Introduction

Welcome to "Hello, Beautiful!" picture books!

This book is about birds. Birds are feathered animals. Each book in the "Hello, Beautiful!" series uses large, colorful photographs and a few words to describe our world to children who are not yet reading on their own or are beginning to learn to read. For the benefit of both grown-up and child readers, a picture key is included in the back of the volume to describe each photograph and specific type of animal in more detail.

"Hello, Beautiful!" books can help pre-readers and starting readers get into the habit of having fun with books and learning from them, too. With pre-readers, a grown-up reader (parent, grandparent, librarian, teacher, older brother or sister) can point to the words on each page as he or she speaks them aloud to help the listening child associate the concept of text with the object or idea it describes.

Large, colorful photographs give pre-readers plenty to see while they listen to the reader. If no reader is available, pre-readers can "read" on their own, turning the pages of the book and speaking their own stories about what they see. For new readers, the photographs provide visual hints about the words on the page. Often, these words describe the specific type of animal shown. This animal may not be representative of all species, or types, of that animal.

This book displays some of the wondrous feathered animals that fly, sing, swim, or waddle throughout the world. Some birds have already become extinct and others are endangered. Help inspire respect and care for these important and beautiful animals by sharing this "Hello, Beautiful!" book with a child soon.

Bluebird

Hello, beautiful bluebird!

You are an eastern bluebird.

Your name tells us that most of your feathers are blue. You are called a songbird because of the kinds of sounds you make.

Cockatoo

Hello, beautiful cockatoo!

You are a sulfur-crested cockatoo.

Like you, most other cockatoos are nearly all white. You have some brightly colored feathers at the back of your head.

Emu

Hello, beautiful emu!

You are a big bird covered in feathers. But you cannot fly! You can run fast on your long legs.

Flamingo

Hello, beautiful flamingo!

You are a greater flamingo.

You live in big groups near lakes and seas. Your feathers can be light pink to bright red.

Heron

Hello, beautiful heron!

You are a great blue heron.

You have long legs and a pointy bill. You use your bill to catch small animals in the water to eat.

Honeyeater

Hello, beautiful honeyeater!

You are a **blue-faced** honeyeater.

You like to sip the sweet juice that flowers make. You have a long tongue that helps you drink.

Osprey

Hello, beautiful osprey!

Flying up high, you watch the water below. Then, you dive into the water and use your feet to catch a fish!

19

Penguin

Hello, beautiful penguin!

You are an emperor penguin.

You can dive and swim fast in the water! Parts of your body look almost like wings. But you cannot fly!

Pheasant

Hello, beautiful pheasant!

You are a golden pheasant.

You have a long tail. Some of your pheasant friends have brightly colored feathers. Others are brown and tan.

Takahē

Hello, beautiful takahē!

Red beak! Orange legs! Shining blue feathers! Bright green feathers!

You cannot fly. Only a few of you are still alive in the world!

Tern

Hello, beautiful tern!

You are an Arctic tern.

You fly...and fly...and fly.

You fly in groups from one end of the world to the other two times a year.

Woodpecker

Hello, beautiful woodpecker!

You are a pileated woodpecker.

You have bright red feathers on the top of your head. You make big holes in trees to live in.

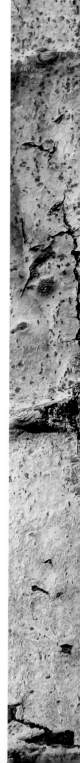

Picture Key

Find out more about these feathered animals! Use the picture keys below to learn where each bird lives, how big it grows, and its favorite foods!

Bluebird

Hello, beautiful bluebird!

You are an eastern bluebird.

Your name tells us that most of your feathers are blue. You are called a songbird because of the kinds of sounds you make.

Cockatoo

Hello, beautiful cockatoo!

You are a sulfur-crested cockatoo.

Like you, most other cockatoos are nearly all white. You have some brightly colored feathers at the back of your head.

Emu

Hello, beautiful emu!

You are a big bird covered in feathers. But you cannot fly! You can run fast on your long legs.

Pages 6-7 Bluebird
The eastern bluebird lives east of the Rocky Mountains from southern Canada to northern Nicaragua. Bluebirds grow to about 7 inches (18 centimeters) long. These birds eat insects and berries.

Pages 8-9 Cockatoo
Sulfur-crested cockatoos (*KOK uh tooz* or *kokuh TOOZ*) live in Australia, New Zealand, and other Pacific islands. They can be from 12 to 24 inches (30 to 60 centimeters) long. They eat nuts, seeds, and fruits.

Pages 10-11 Emu
The emu (*EE myoo*) lives in Australia. Adult emus stand about 5 ½ feet (1.7 meters) high. Emus eat fruits and plants.

Flamingo

Hello, beautiful flamingo!

You are a greater flamingo.

You live in big groups near lakes and seas. Your feathers can be light pink to bright red.

Heron

Hello, beautiful heron!

You are a great blue heron.

You have long legs and a pointy bill. You use your bill to catch small animals in the water to eat.

Honeyeater

Hello, beautiful honeyeater!

You are a blue-faced honeyeater.

You like to sip the sweet juice that flowers make. You have a long tongue that helps you drink.

Pages 12-13 Flamingo
The greater flamingo (*fluh MIHNG goh*) lives in parts of Africa, southern Asia, and southern Europe. These birds stand from 3 to 5 feet (91 to 150 centimeters) tall. Flamingos eat shellfish and small plantlike living things called *algae* (*AL jee*).

Pages 14-15 Heron
The great blue heron (*HEHR uhn*) lives in North America. It can grow from 3 to 4.5 feet (91 to 137 centimeters) from head to tail. Herons like to eat fish, frogs, and crayfish.

Pages 16-17 Honeyeater
The blue-faced honeyeater lives in Australia and parts of New Guinea. These birds are 10 to 12 inches (26 to 32 centimeters) long. They eat insects, fruits, and the sweet juice made by flowers called *nectar*.

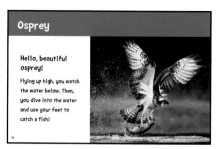

Pages 18-19 Osprey
Ospreys *(OS preez)* live near rivers, lakes, seacoasts, and bays around the world. Most of these birds grow to about 2 feet (60 centimeters) long. The wings can be three times as long as the bird's body. It hunts and eats fish.

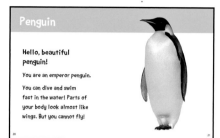

Pages 20-21 Penguin
The emperor penguin *(PEHN gwihn)* is the largest of all penguins. It grows up to 3 feet (1 meter) tall. Emperor penguins live in Antarctica. They catch fish, *krill* (a kind of shellfish), and squid to eat.

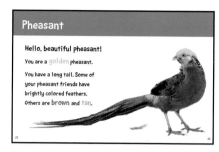

Pages 22-23 Pheasant
The golden pheasant *(FEHZ uhnt)* lives in central China. An adult male will be from 35 to 41 inches (90 to 105 centimeters) long. The tail is the longest part of the bird. These pheasants eat seeds, fruits, and insects.

Pages 24-25 Takahē
The takahē *(tah KAH hay)* lives only in New Zealand. They grow to about 20 inches (50 centimeters) tall. Takahēs eat seeds and plants.

Pages 26-27 Tern
For half the year, the Arctic tern lives near the northern part of the Atlantic Ocean. Then it flies to the waters of Antarctica to live for the rest of the year. The birds grow to about 17 inches (43 centimeters) long. They eat small fish.

Pages 28-29 Woodpecker
The pileated *(PY lee AY tihd* or *PIHL ee AY tihd)* woodpecker lives in the United States and Canada. These birds grow from 16 to 19 inches (40 to 49 centimeters) long. Woodpeckers eat insects.

Index